• Edward D Lavieri Jr. •

Software
Consulting

A Revolutionary Approach

DEDICATIONS

Dedicated to all the budding software consultants in the world. This is one of the best gigs in the world. If you want to be part of it, you can.

To Maria—my bride of twenty-five years. Without her understanding and compassion, you would not be holding this book.

ACKNOWLEDGEMENTS

Special thanks goes to Jenny at CreateSpace for her patience and guiding hand, Doug and Scott for getting me started, and to the brilliant folks in Edinburgh, Scotland. Thank you all.

TABLE OF CONTENTS

Chapter 5 - Software Development

Chapter 6 - What Else You Should Know

INTRODUCTION

Congratulations! Since you are reading this book, you have taken the first step in the process of becoming a successful software consultant. There are so many of us, we should have our own union. Not to worry, this book will give you the insights and, more importantly, the confidence you need to be successful. There really is room for all of us in this space.

This book is intended for individuals and small teams that want to start their own software consulting business. Consultants that have recently started and those that want to increase their efficiency and income stand to benefit from this book as well. The book was written because often times in this business, there is no one to ask the types of questions this book answers. Other consultants might see you as a potential competitor and, therefore, will not want to help you.

While this book was written with a purposeful content flow, each chapter building upon the previous chapter(s), there is no harm in jumping around to focus on what is most important to you. One of the key features of this book is a running case study that appears at the end of each chapter. This real world case study demonstrates how the concepts in the book can be applied.

Let's take a brief look at the chapters in this book. Chapter 1 is the introductory chapter, but that does not mean it is light on content. We start with a look at the transition to the world of consulting and try to determine if you are likely to be successful. Other topics include a review of some benefits and detractors of being a consultant. Then, we detail the importance of having a strategic plan and provide you with some examples. The chapter concludes, as promised, with Part I of our Case Study.

With **Chapter 2**, we start getting into the real nuts and bolts of establishing your consultancy business. A six-step approach is used, which starts with (1) finding your niche. Following steps are: (2) Creating Your Identity, (3) Assembling Your Team and Network, (4) Establishing Your Budget, (5) Developing a Pricing Model, and (6) Marketing Yourself. This chapter takes you from start to finish in getting your business set up. As you have already come to expect, the chapter ends with Part II of our Case Study.

In **Chapter 3**, we focus on your clients. Since they are consultants' source of revenue, we need to learn how to find them, give them what they want (sometimes), generate return business from them, and grow our business by obtaining a steady flow of new clients. Part III of our Case Study concludes the chapter.

Chapter 4 is all about tools we can use to ensure our business and business processes are efficient. This chapter does not merely review tools you can use (many are free); it also gives you insights and guides on how to use them efficiently. In addition to technology tools, you will learn key concepts in managing yourself in your new role as a consultant. The next installment, Part IV, of our Case Study will help you increase your efficiency and productivity—saving time and money is not a bad thing.

Chapter 5 covers software development from theoretical and procedural standpoints. It is in this chapter that the meaning of the book's byline, "A Revolutionary Approach," is realized. You are not going to believe what you read, but trust me, it is all true. If you only read one section of this book, be sure to read where the secret to the Revolutionary Approach is unveiled. Of course, I hope you will read the entire book and refer to it afterwards. This chapter's Case Study, Part V, is especially valuable in that it provides concrete examples of the Revolutionary Approach.

Our final chapter, **Chapter 6**, presents a few topics that are not often found in consultancy books. Having to learn the hard way about parts of your business that are critical—such as legal and tax issues—can take the fun out of being a consultant. We will avoid that by covering those topics here.

You will find a glossary at the end of the book with a list of acronyms and terminology used in this book.

Okay, you are ready to start reading **Chapter 1**. Enjoy.

CHAPTER ONE

GETTING STARTED

Being a consultant is not for everyone, and for those that are suited for such a job, not all are able to do it as a full-time profession. Reviewing your potential for this field will either save you a lot of money and heartache or provide you with requisite confidence to start your career as a software consultant.

Although there are seven basic types of software consultants—programmers, application developers, system designers/engineers, solution specialists, Web developers, database specialists, and network engineers—there are other types of software consultants and many types within each major category. For the sake of organization, we will highlight the seven basic types listed above. Knowing what expertise you have and how it fits into the software consulting field is an important step toward realizing your goal.

When companies and organizations face a software-related problem outside of their staff's abilities, the answer is often, "Let's hire an expert." You want to be that expert, so let's get started in getting you to that point.

YOU AS A CONSULTANT

So, you are thinking about becoming a consultant, providing consultations to individuals, businesses, governmental agencies, and not-for-profit organizations based on your unique experience, talent, and abilities. You are probably asking yourself questions: Do I really have something unique to offer?

Is there anyone out there willing to pay for what I know or what I can do? Will I be able to make a decent living as a software consultant?

These important questions need to be addressed. Going into anything half-heartedly or without sufficient research and analysis is sure to end in less than ideal results. Any job change is sure to add stress to your life as well as conflicting emotions like excitement, uncertainty, inspiration, apprehension, and confidence. Financial considerations are often at the heart of making the decision of whether or not to step away from your comfort zone and become a software consultant. Therefore, it is recommended that you prepare a detailed budget that covers the previous year. This laborious process will help ensure you have a firm grasp of your expenditures. Here are the steps in the budgetary process:

- Document all expenditures from the previous year.
- Organize your expenditures into categories that make sense to you. Some suggestions are:
  - Mortgage / rent
  - Utilities
  - Food (ensure you include meals and beverages consumed outside of your home)
  - Entertainment (include home cable / satellite service, movies, DVDs, etc.)
  - Communications (this includes services such as home phone, cell phone plans, and Internet access)
  - Clothing
  - Medical / dental expenses
  - Insurance (home, auto, life, medical, and dental)
  - Automobile loans, gas, and upkeep
  - Childcare
  - Savings / investments
  - Charity
  - Vacations

- ☐ Holiday gift giving
- ☐ Magazines and other periodicals
- ☐ Other categories that make sense for your life
- Total your yearly budget and add 10 percent to create an inflation-safe buffer.
- Determine how much income you need to maintain your current lifestyle. This amount will be your minimum net income target for your new consultancy business.

Whenever switching jobs, especially to one with an unsure source of income, it is a good idea to ensure you have ample savings to provide for your planned expenses for a period of time. Having enough savings to cover expenses in between jobs is a smart precautionary measure. This gives you the opportunity to build your consultancy business without the pressure of finding immediate income. It also prevents you from taking on projects and clients that you would not normally want. Consulting a professional accountant or a financial expert at your bank or credit union is a great way to ensure you do not make costly mistakes.

What characteristics should you have to ensure your success as a consultant? You do not necessarily need to be an evangelist or smooth talker; rather, you should have certain competencies:

- Ability to articulate your expertise and solutions
- Some level of expertise in a given area (this is your core competency)
- Ability to collaborate with others
- Flexibility, especially when dealing with clients and collaborators in time zones other than your own
- Technical aptitude (more on this later)
- Ability to communicate via various methods (more on this later)

Most of all, you should be passionate about the area of consulting you plan to enter. If you lack this passion, you might as well put this book down and keep your current job. Your heart and mind really have to be committed to your decision to become a software consultant. Moreover, if you have a spouse, s/he should be supportive of your decision.

REAPING THE BENEFITS

Once your software consulting business is up and running, you will start to enjoy certain benefits that are not normally possible with your typical 9-to-5 job.

One of the most important benefits is known as the WLG Balance. This is a harmonious balance between your Work, Life, and Goals. For perhaps the first time, you will be in control of what your work consists of. You will also be able to capitalize on life situations such as taking part of family holidays and vacations. Balancing your work and life will help you meet your overall goals for your life and work.

A more concrete benefit is the ability to set your own hours, decide what days you want to work, and take time off when you want. Your clients might have some say in this and, since they are paying you, that is OK. That being said, you can still set aside days that you do not take meetings, even if it is a weekend day. Having at least one complete day each week without meetings ensures you have time to strategize, research, and plan.

Once you have a sufficient stream of income or war chest, you can turn down jobs that you are not interested in. This is not something you likely experienced working that regular 9-to-5 job. This freedom is one of the guilty pleasures of being your own boss.

Have you ever been in a work environment where they had *casual Fridays, no-tie Wednesdays*, or some other unceremonious relaxed business attire day periodically? Unless you are meeting clients in person or having video meetings, every day is casual as a consultant—another guilty pleasure.

Most consultants work from home, at least in the early stages of their consultant life. This represents several different benefits. First, you save yourself commuting time and expenses, wear and tear on your vehicle, and frustrating traffic. Working at home provides added security to your home, which can be important in some areas. Another benefit from working at home is you do not have to go out to lunch or bring your lunch to work.

AVOIDING THE POTHOLES

The road to a successful software consultancy business is peppered with potholes. As long as you know what to expect of the road ahead, these potholes are easily avoidable.

One of the most common potholes new consultants, entrepreneurs, and other start-ups fall into is letting work consume them. It is common for these folks to work eighteen to twenty-four months straight without ever taking a day off. While some might argue this is a necessary part of starting your own business, others will tell you this can cause burnout, decrease efficiency, degrade your health, and ultimately be the downfall of your business. Only you can decide at what level you must work to get your consultancy up and running. If you have partners or employees, you should ensure they do not fall into this pothole.

In the previous section, I sang the praises of working at home. This can also be a pothole. Depending on your home situation, the number of interruptions might be excessive. Imagine being on a videoconference with a high-profile client when your spouse

walks in wearing pajamas or having your young children scream-
ing in the background. This does not present a professional image,
so you will want to avoid these types of interruptions. The best
situation is to have a room away from common areas in the house
to conduct your business, or at least your meetings. Having your
own phone line is important as well since you do not want anyone
in the house to pick up the phone and start dialing when you are
on an important call.

Being at home can result in undue distractions. While talking
mental and physical breaks from your work is important, this can
be overdone. The "Honey Do List" and home projects that are
undone might attract your attention when you should be working.
This can be difficult for some people, so scheduling that time is a
good way to avoid the dreaded home distraction pothole.

ASSESSING YOUR POTENTIAL

So far, we have looked at some of the requirements, benefits, and
potholes that you will encounter. Now is a good time to consider
seriously if you have a chance at this. Such an assessment requires research, self-reflection, and honesty. Let's look at each of
these three elements as distinct steps in the process of assessing
your potential.

STEP 1: RESEARCH. You need to determine what your
niche will be (this is detailed in Chapter 2). Conduct research to
determine what businesses and consultants are in that same niche.
You can start with Internet searches, reading blogs and trade
magazines, and reviewing business directories. Once you have a
feel for who else is already doing what you want to do, look at
the types of customers they have, try to determine how much the
charge, and see what their products look like. What you are doing
is researching your competition and getting an idea of what services are currently available.

STEP 2: SELF-REFLECTION. Can you do what your competitors are doing? You do not have to be as good, cheap, or quick as your competitors, but you should bring something attractive to the fight. Rest assured, this business is increasingly competitive. Do you possess the six characteristics listed in the "You as a Consultant" section?

STEP 3: HONESTY. This step refers to the need to be honest with yourself. When starting your own consultancy, there is no time for self-doubt or a lack of confidence. Are you committed to making this work? After analyzing your research, reviewing the self-reflection points from Step 2, and taking a detailed look at your budget, ask yourself if you are suited to be a software consultant.

Developing a Strategic Plan

The purpose of a strategic plan is to provide your business with a set of guiding principles that define and guide your business. As a general rule, all aspects of your strategic plan should be clear and concise. Creating a strategic plan requires a lot of thought and can be broken down into five basic steps.

STEP 1: CREATE A MISSION STATEMENT. What is the mission of your business? This is your business' overall goal. Some aspects to consider when developing your mission statement:

- Your business' ethical or moral values
- A brief description of the services your consultancy will provide
- Identification of your target customer base

Example: To provide innovative software solutions to government agencies, businesses, and non-profit organizations.

STEP 2: DOCUMENT YOUR VALUE. Document what unique value you can provide to your clients that your competitors cannot.

STEP 3: CREATE A VISION STATEMENT. Consider what you want your business to be like in five to ten years. Will you enter new markets or expand your service offerings? Perhaps you will launch an industry-leading software application. These are long-term goals that you can refer back to and work toward.

STEP 4: SWOT ANALYSIS. This is the traditional strategic management tool where you analyze your business potential by looking at Strengths, Weaknesses, Opportunities, and Threats. If this is new to you, it might be a good idea to review a strategic management textbook at your local library.

STEP 5: CUSTOMER IDENTIFICATION. In this step, you should establish your intended customer base. This can change over time, but it is important to establish who your initial intended customers are. The more details you document in this step, the better prepared you will be for obtaining your intended customers.

This five-step approach to strategic planning is an abbreviated one. More detailed strategic planning methodologies are available. It is your plan, so you can add and remove elements as you see fit. Once you establish your plan, you should periodically review and update it. Most importantly, you should model your business after it.

CASE STUDY: PART I

This is the first part of a continuing case study that is featured at the end of each chapter. The examples provided in the case study are from my actual experiences. Your results will likely be different and, hopefully even more successful than mine.

As way of introduction, I joined the United States Navy as a young adult and retired after twenty-five years of active service. During my time in the Navy, my passion for computers and, more specifically, computer programming grew. Whenever possible, I found ways to incorporate computers into my work and even developed a few applications along the way. In between long sea duty assignments and deployments, I worked on college degrees to improve my programming skills and knowledge of information systems. After retirement, I decided to start my own consulting business with hopes of working as an instructional designer, computer programmer, and information systems specialist.

As detailed in this chapter, financial concerns were at the forefront of my decision to become a software consultant. This decision was made with my wife, who had been with me for twenty-four of my twenty-five years in the Navy. My Navy pension, my wife's income, and income from my adjunct faculty jobs enabled me to develop my consultancy business at my own pace. At first, teaching provided a financial crutch for me, one that I enjoyed. To this day, I continue to teach, but not for financial security. Rather, I teach because I enjoy connecting with learners and helping them in their academic journeys.

Under the category of Reaping the Benefits, I ensured that all my meetings with clients were in the middle of the week. Fortunately, I was able to schedule the courses I taught the same way. This resulted in 3-day workweek with a weekly 4-day weekend. Of course I did do some work during my long weekends, but only because I wanted to. When you love your work, you do not mind doing it on the weekends.

It was important for me to have a quiet place to work and conduct my meetings. We converted the second floor of our house into an office. This 36 x 16 room even had its own bathroom, so I was set. Early on, I had interruptions from family at inopportune times, so I purchased a reversible Open/Closed sign and put it on my door. After that time, my family could look at the sign from the bottom of the stairs. This worked like magic (and still does to this day).

Chapter Two

Six Steps to Creation

The previous chapter was aimed at helping you make the decision as to **if** you should become a software consultant. This chapter helps you get started by exploring **how** to become a software consultant.

Step 1: Finding Your Niche

A niche refers to a specific segment of a market. The smaller the niche, the greater the opportunity will be for new entrants to have success. Even though the number of independent software consultants and consulting firms is large, there are still plenty of niches ripe for your business. The task of finding your niche involves two primary functions: research and selection.

Research

The research phase involves determining how the market is segmented into niches as well as how crowded or sparsely populated the niches are. There is no single or standard method of segmenting the software consulting market. You can take one of several approaches, including segmenting the market by product, customer, content, and method. Let's take a brief look at each of these approaches.

Product segmentation divides the market based on product categories such as databases, learning management systems, content management systems, knowledge management systems, decision support systems, inventory systems, business-to-business systems, business-to-consumer systems, eLearning, eGames, social networking, productivity, 2D, 3D, consumer-to-consumer systems, animation, engineering, enterprise resource systems, and more. This list is certainly not exhaustive, but it should give you an idea how to cull out types of products to create categories. If you are a pure programmer, you might have a hard time narrowing down the types of products you advertise and develop. Clients usually like to see sample applications that closely resemble what they are hiring you to do. If you are unable to narrow your focus, it will be challenging to show expertise in any single area. This is a business of expertise, so it is important to find a niche and thoroughly develop its related competencies.

Customer segmentation is the easiest method of market division. Categories can be very broad such as government and non-government. That level of segmentation is usually not sufficient; rather, a more narrow market division is required. Example categories include government agencies, military branches, not-for-profit organizations, academia, small businesses, publishers, retailers, kiosk owners, restaurants, and so on. This list can be virtually limitless which should be encouraging for those looking for a niche.

Content segmentation is a common approach resulting in many software consultants specializing in a single content area. These content areas are varied and do not follow any standardized categorization. Examples include common academic areas such as mathematics, social studies, sciences, geography, nutrition, health, and history. These academic areas can be further divided into academic levels (i.e., primary school, secondary school, post-secondary school, and graduate school). Other content areas that software consultants have specialized in include finance, foreign languages, physical security, medicine, computer security, ethics, public safety, industrial safety, politics, public policy, biometrics, entertainment, sales, automotive, communications, legal, business, fashion, marketing, and broadcasting. As with the previous segmentation approaches, this list is representative of the possible categories you could specialize in.

Methodology segmentation is an approach that focuses on the technological methods or tools you use in your software consultancy. Examples can include specific programming languages (e.g., JavaScript, C#, PHP) and delivery platforms (e.g., Windows, Mac, Linux, iPod, other mobile devices, and the Web). It is common for some clients to require a specific language for their projects. This requirement is sometimes unwarranted, but in other cases, it is because the client desires the ability to modify applications easily post-delivery/deployment.

Determining how to segment the market is only the first part of the research phase of finding your niche. The next step is to determine if the niche you are most interested in is crowded or sparsely populated with consultants. There are several ways to make this determination. One method would be to conduct Web searches to determine how many results you get. Most software consultants will have an established Web presence, so they should not be difficult to find. Searching for blogs is another method. Many consultants maintain their own blogs as an advertising effort. To find these blogs, you can conduct advanced searches with your favorite search engine or check blog registries.

Selection

Once you have fully researched potential market segments you are interested in and have an idea of how dense the pool of consultants are for those areas, you are ready to make a decision. You have a few options open to you: select a single market; select a single sub-section of a market; select multiple markets; select multiple sub-sections of one market; or select multiple sub-sections of multiple markets. It is common for software consultants to select a broad market segment as their niche, but to their downfall. Large consultancies can get away with specializing in a large market segment, but it is very difficult and, in fact, nearly impossible, for an independent software consultant to pull this off.

If you are starting your software consulting business with only a few people or even just yourself, it is more advisable that you find a very specific market segment as your niche. Combining segments to create a specialized niche will likely help reduce the number of competitors you have. To combine segments, you simply select a segment from two or more of the approaches previously discussed in the research section of finding a niche. Some examples of combined segment niches are:

- Role-Playing Ethics Simulations
- Mobile Phone Financial Applications
- 2D History eLearning modules
- Open-Source Content Management Systems
- iPod Applications for Kiosk Owners
- 3D Foreign Language eGames

This is a very short list, but the possibilities are only limited to your imagination, knowledge, and abilities.

STEP 2: CREATING YOUR IDENTITY

Several aspects of your consultancy need careful planning. First, you need to make a decision as to what your business will be called. You might just use your name such as John Doe Consulting or select a business name such as ABC Consulting or Red Star Consulting. You should ensure that the name you select is appropriate for the market segment you selected in Step 1 (Finding Your Niche). For example, you might be tempted to name your company after your favorite dog breed such as Irish Setter Consulting. While that is a great name, it might not help you land consulting jobs with government or health agencies. It is possible that the name of your business could prevent you from getting certain jobs.

So, spend quality time on this step. Once you select and advertise your name, it may not be feasible to make a change. If this situation should arise, you have options available to you. First, you could simply change the name and ensure your clients are advised, Web sites are changed, business accounts and subscriptions are updated, business cards and letterhead is changed, and... you get the idea. This can be tough. Another option is to establish a sub-company or name an arm of your business as a "Doing Business As" (DBA), which will afford you certain legal rights. If your original company was Silver Lining Consulting LLC, you could then create a DBA named, "Silver eLearning" and tout it as "Silver eLearning, a Silver Lining Consulting company." The best bet, of course, is to pick your initial name wisely so that you do not have to worry about this mess.

Now that your consultancy business has a name, you are ready to make your name available to the public. There are a number of approaches to this including creating a Web site (a must), logo design, professional email address, official phone line or lines, social networking, and advertising. Before we look at each of those "going public" approaches, you must first have a firm grasp of what your consultancy does and how it does it.

Web Site

There are four essential elements of Web sites for your business: domain name, hosting, content, and maintenance. Each of these elements is important; not one is more important than the others. Just like other elements of establishing your business, your foray into establishing a Web presence requires thoughtful planning and, in many cases, research.

Selecting a domain name, the name of your on-line identify, is not terribly difficult, but it is terribly important. The best possible case is that your company's name is available as a domain. For example, if your company was Violet Finger Consulting, you might want to register the domain, www.violetfinger.com; which, at the time this book was written, was available. What do you do if your business name is not available as a domain? You could change from a dot com address to a dot net (e.g., www.violetfinger.net), but the business world expects you to have a dot com address. Now you are left with two options: (1) change the name of your company, or (2) change the name of your domain. Ideally, you will search for a company name and check for domain name availability at the same time. If your name is already set and the similar domain name is taken, you might search for an alternative (e.g., www.vfc.com for Violet Finger Consulting).

Congratulations. You now have your domain name. Now it is time to move on to the second element—hosting. Unless you are an IT guru and have your own servers directly connected to the Internet, you are going to need the assistance of a hosting provider. There are many very good solutions out there, with the industry leaders advertising via television, radio, printed periodicals, and Internet pod and video casts. Here are things you should look at when shopping for a hosting company:

- Technical Capability. Does the company offer the technical server-side features you need? Will you need a Windows or Linux server? Not sure, call the company. If they are not willing to talk to you about your needs (even if you are not sure about them), then they do not deserve your money.
- Scalability. It is usually frugal to start small when it comes to Web hosting. Many companies have easy scalability options for you. Again, ask about this before you make your decision. You want your hosting service to grow with your company.

- Customer Support. This is extremely important and should be available to you in two forms. First, there should be ample online quick-start guides, how-tos, and procedure manuals. Secondly, the hosting service should provide 24/7 customer support via phone. I do not recommend selecting a service that does not offer 24/7 support. If your site is down at 2:00 am on Saturday, you are not going to want to wait for "normal business hours" on Monday.
- Bandwidth. Review the bandwidth capacities to ensure the company supports your current and future needs. Again—I know you see this coming—talk to the provider before making your final decision.
- Email Addresses. You are going to want professional domain-specific email accounts (e.g., ed@yourcompanyname.com (if your name is Ed)). As your company grows, you might need multiple accounts. Most providers sell additional email accounts in blocks, so up-scaling is not difficult or too costly. Even in the short term, you will likely want more than one email account. This is true even if you are a one-person company. Examples include: info@yourcompanyname.com; contact@yourcompanyname.com; sales@yourcompanyname.com, etc.). Another email feature that the hosting provider you select should offer is a "catch-all" email account. This feature allows you to assign one of your email accounts as a "catch-all," meaning that an email is sent to your domain (e.g., @yourcompanynme.com) that does not have a corresponding email account (e.g., ceo@yourcompanyname.com), you can have it routed to the "catch-all" account. This ensures your company will not miss any emails.

- **Control Panel.** Professional hosting companies will have a control panel that serves as the software interface between you and your server. Most of these are pretty standard, but it might be worth asking for a sneak peak at it to ensure it looks user-friendly.
- **Statistical Reporting.** Hosting companies certainly have access to and collect Web traffic. How much of that you have access to and for how much money is dependent upon the norms of the hosting company you select. Some of these companies will even auto-email you monthly/quarterly user statistics. Here it is again...contact the hosting company to see what your options are and how much each of them costs.

Selecting content for your Web site is not something that can be covered in great detail in a book such as this. Consulting companies are unique entities, each with unique content requirements. What can be said about content in a broad, generic approach is that it should have the following characteristics:

- Relevancy
- Professionalism
- Free of errors
- Easy to navigate
- Up-to-date

The fourth essential element of your Web presence is Maintenance. The number one pitfall of small (and some large) companies is that they spend a lot of time developing their Web site, just to leave it dormant for long periods of time. This is not a fire-once-and-forget ordeal. You must make sure your Web site is periodically updated, or you will most assuredly turn some potential clients away.

Logo

Most people learn well by visual association. How many company logos can you identify? I bet the answer is "a lot." Media bombards us with logos and other imagery. Now it is your turn. Creating a simple but professional logo can exponentially increase the credibility and professional look of your business. If you open your favorite Web browser and type "logo design" into a search engine, you will be amazed at how many services are available. For a very small investment, you can be presented with several logo drafts that are appropriate for your business.

Some of the providers have a very quick turnaround time and, once you select the final artwork, provide your logo to you in multiple formats.

Email

We previously discussed the minimum requirements regarding email accounts that your hosting company should provide. So, now that you have an email account associated with your business, use it. Do not fall into the trap of using your personal email accounts for business, especially free services. This can communicate a lack of professionalism, disorganization, and generally give potential or current clients an uneasy feeling.

It should go without saying that a professional signature block should be used for all company emails. Also off the "no-brainer" list: ensure there are no typos, be professional, only include graphics or attachments if necessary, start with an appropriate salutation, and end with an appropriate closing. It is worth a few seconds for each email to ensure they are properly addressed. Do not include personnel on the email unless they need to receive it. Lastly, stay away from blind-copying people on your emails. Think about this—it could come back to bite you.

Phone

At some point, you are going to need to receive business-related phone calls. Do you give out your home phone and take a chance that your teenage daughter answers the phone in a manner in which you would not want to expose your clients? This is not advisable. Do you provide your mobile number? If you do, then you will want to take a couple of precautions:

- Always answer the phone in a professional manner, such as "This is Ed, how may I help you?" Unless you are 100 percent sure the caller is your spouse, you should never answer the phone, "Hi honey." If you can avoid these pitfalls, then using your personal mobile number might be an option.
- Secondly, use a professional voice mail recording. Instead of, "I am out, hit me back," or "This is Ed, you know what to do," use something like:
    - "You have reached the voicemail of <name>. I am currently out of the office or on another line. Please leave your name, number, and a brief message. I will get back to you as soon as possible."
    - "Violet Finger Consulting. We cannot come to the phone right now...."
    - "Hi, this is <name>, the Violet Finger <title>. I am currently unavailable...."

Using a professional voice mail service is another option. Some of them have 24/7 live-human access. Where they merely take down the information and electronically provide it to you. This is not a bad option, but the service will know little to nothing about your business particulars.

Social Networking

Social networking sites are home to millions of users every day. The inclusion of them in this step (Creating your Identity) is not a recommendation to use them, rather, acknowledgement that it makes sense for some companies. Only you will know if you can benefit from establishing a corporate presence on one or more of these sites. Most of them have free profiles so it might not cost you any money, only time.

If you decide to establish a presence on one or more of the social networking sites, research their patronage first. What are the demographics of their patrons? Do they match your target audience? These questions are worth investigating.

Advertising

The final part of creating your identity is to invest in advertising, if it makes sense for you to do so. Some software consulting companies acquire their first client without advertising and that client provides them enough work to keep them fully occupied. In this scenario, advertising would likely draw in additional clients you would have to turn down. You will know when and if the time is right to advertise.

If you decide to advertise your business, there are a couple of areas you can target. Keep in mind that you want to think about reaching your specific target audience. So, your advertising decisions will largely be based on your target audience.

- eMagazines
- Blogs
- Industry journals
- Trade magazines
- Conferences

Okay, that wraps it up for Step 2. Be warned; the effects of poor initial execution is difficult to overcome. What does this mean and how does it apply to creating your identity? Use sufficient time, mental energy, and research before selecting a name for your company, your Web domain, a logo, your email accounts, phone service, social networking site presence, and advertising. You know the saying, "a pound of preparation...."

STEP 3: ASSEMBLING YOUR TEAM AND NETWORK

Most software consulting companies start with one or two people, usually, just one. You might be okay on your own for a while, but if you have even the slightest modicum of success, you will need help. If you are a pure programmer, you might need a graphic artist, translator, voice-over expert, animator, 3D modeler, subject-matter-expert, and more. Unless you land a huge contract or are independently wealthy, you will probably not be able to afford full-time employees, at least not in the beginning.

Finding work-for-hire freelancers / contractors is not difficult. There are online services where you can post a project (for free) and attract bids from multiple freelancers / contractors. The cost of these sites is usually bore by the freelancer / contractor, not the employer (you). You will read more about these online services in Chapter 4. Alternatively, you can post job postings on your Web site.

The Internet makes it possible for you to think globally about your team composition. There are very talented people all over the world. You are not relegated to using ones only from your country. The best is not always the most expensive, but the most expensive is almost always not the best. Look outside your borders for additional options.

You should consult a tax attorney and/or accountant before hiring a freelancer / contractor. They will help make sure your actions are in accordance with local and federal laws. Also, knowing what to expect at tax time can prevent undue stress and legal problems.

Once you start working with other people (e.g., graphic artist) you are likely to find ones you work with well. They quickly become part of your network. This is a situation of consultants helping consultants. The stronger your network, the more efficient your processes will be and your time and cost estimates will become increasingly more accurate.

STEP 4: ESTABLISHING YOUR BUDGET

While this step is fourth in line, it does not mean that you should not have thought about financial matters early on. Certainly, if you cannot afford to go into business for yourself, you would not be reading this book. So, this step is not concerned if you can afford this business; rather, it focuses on how to budget your operations.

The costs of establishing and running a software consulting business are not astronomical. Most recurring fees are small enough not to give the entrepreneur pause. Unchecked, however, these fees can add up. The following lists contain typical startup, recurring, and non-periodic fees. Prices are not mentioned because they vary and can be easily obtained via a standard Web search.

Start-up Fees

- LLC or incorporation fees
- Trademark / service mark filing

- Charter review (attorney)
- Tax advice (accountant)
- Hardware, software, furniture, and supply acquisition

Recurring Fees

- Domain renewal
- Hosting services
- Phone line / service contract
- Internet service
- Online meeting / collaboration subscriptions
- Voice-mail service
- Fax service
- Trade magazine / eZine subscriptions
- Professional profile fees (social networking)
- Cloud computing fees
- Quarterly income tax
- Software renewals (e.g., anti-virus)

Non-Periodic Fees

- Conference fees
- Advertising
- Outsourcing (e.g., graphic artist)
- Hardware replacement / upgrades
- Software purchases
- Travel

These are just the typical fees you will encounter. Your business will be unique, so you are likely to have unique costs. Purchasing a small-business accounting software package is likely to help you keep track of these expenses. Starting your business with one of these software packages is highly advisable. Playing catch-up later is tough. Your accountant will thank you.

STEP 5: DEVELOPING A PRICING MODEL

So, how much do you charge? How much are you worth? Believe it or not, these two questions are not always related to one another. We cannot always charge what we are worth, at least not at first. A plethora of software developers and consultants over-seas provide their services for very cheap; many well under $10 per hour. Guess what? They are very good at what they do. Do not let this dissuade you. Your experience and approach will be completely different than anyone else out there.

You might have to under bid on a couple of initial projects to get your feet wet. This is a quick and easy way to demonstrate that you have previous work. Not many clients are going to sign up to be your first customer. If you take this advice, then limit these initial jobs to small ones. After all, you do not want to lock yourself into a low-paying contact that is going to take up a lot of your time.

There are two primary pricing models in the software consult-ing and software development businesses: hourly rate and fixed price. You should become adept at both models because different clients will require different models. Some clients will request quotes using both models. There are advantages and disadvan-tages to both models. Let's look at both of them now.

Hourly Rate

If you use this model, then you will need to have a firm grip on the hourly rates for each of your team members (internal and external) and how many hours of work they will perform for the entire project. This level of granularity is only possible after thorough review of the work. Hopefully this work is defined in a *Design Specification Document*. Do not hesitate to enter into a dialogue with the potential client before offering a bid. Failure to bid on a project you do not clearly understand or that has a poorly defined scope will likely cost you more than you get paid.

Here is a typical breakout of the Hourly Rates. Keep in mind that these rates are not industry standard, but they are ones I have used.

Employee	Rate	Hours	Total Fee
Lead Programmer	$50	100	$5,000
Animator	$35	30	$1,050
Instructional Designer	$40	40	$1,600
Graphic Artist	$25	20	$ 500
Tester	$20	15	$ 300
Management	$42	16	$ 672

The total for this project would be $9,122. For a total project time of 221 hours, the overall hourly rate would be $41.28. That just takes care of your direct labor costs. Under the hour rate method of pricing, it is typical to add a markup on the hourly rate, which accounts for your profit. At a basic level, you can simply mark-up up the overall hourly rate. For example, if you added a 20% markup on the rate of $41.28, the new rate becomes $49.54. Using this model, you earn greater profits from lower wage earners. Depending upon how much you use each wage earner during the project, your profit margin could shrink or grow. If our time estimate is accurate (221 hours), your client will pay $10,948.34 for a slim profit margin of $1,826.34.

You can build a more complex mark-up model by individually marking up hourly wages. As illustrated in the next table, the markups do not have to be standard.

Employee	Rate	Markup	New Rate	Hours	Total Fee
Lead Programmer	$50	10%	$55	100	$5,500
Animator	$35	15%	$40	30	$1,200
Instructional Designer	$40	0%	$40	40	$1,600
Graphic Artist	$25	20%	$30	20	$ 600
Tester	$20	20%	$24	15	$ 360
Management	$42	20%	$50	16	$ 800

This more complex version results in a total price of $10,060, which equates to an hourly rate of $45.52. Since your direct labor costs were $9,122, your profit is $938. While this is not an ideal situation, it gives you an idea of how this model works.

New clients are not likely to be in favor of an hourly rate quote. Their primary concern is cost overruns. They typically have a budget for a specific project and want to ensure it can be done for that amount or less. That is where the more common fixed price model comes in.

Fixed Price

The Fixed Price model is easy for clients to grasp and accept. This is simple for them. They have a project and you say you can get it done for a specific amount. That amount is within their project budget, so the contract is signed. If you go over budget, that is your problem. If you go under budget, that is your profit. This is not to suggest that you should overbid on projects, but you will want some working room.

This model is easy for you as the service provider, but requires you to have sound project planning and management skills. Projects can quickly get out of hand and cost you more than you are being paid. Let's look at how to determine what your fixed price bid should be using our previous example.

Here is our original table. Based on your project planning and estimating, you determine that the project will require the services of six personnel with differing wages. The total cost to you, before profit, is $9,122.

Employee	Rate	Hours	Total Fee
Lead Programmer	$50	100	$5,000
Animator	$35	30	$1,050
Instructional Designer	$40	40	$1,600
Graphic Artist	$25	20	$ 500
Tester	$20	15	$ 300
Management	$42	16	$ 672

To incorporate profit and room for estimating errors, you will add a markup on the total price.

Markup %	New Total	Profit
10%	$10,034	$ 912
15%	$10,490	$1,368
20%	$10,946	$1,824
25%	$11,403	$2,281
30%	$11,859	$2,737

When determining a markup percentage you should consider fairness and competitiveness.

STEP 6: MARKETING YOURSELF

This step is a follow-up to Step 2 (Creating Your Identity). In Step 2, you created a public image for your company, one that potential clients can see, research, and learn about. You need to market yourself. Whether you like it or not, you are your company. Your personality and reputation can help your company earn more business and grow into new markets. Each contact you make at conferences, seminars, professional chat rooms, and clients are part of your network. Keep those network nodes alive so that you will be remembered.

This is outside the comfort zone for many people. If you are uncomfortable with this, buy a book on self-confidence, building your network, or marketing yourself. There are many great books on those topics, so we will not cover them here. Nonetheless, this is an important step.

CASE STUDY: PART II

Our case study continues. In Part II, I detail successes and lessons learned that I experienced in each of the six steps covered in this chapter.

Step 1: Finding Your Niche

This was initially a difficult task for me. I knew I wanted to be a programmer but was unsure how to break in. I was working on my third graduate degree at the time I started my software consulting business. That degree would become a MS in Education with a specialization (major) in Instructional Design. Based on that, and that alone, I decided on the niche of eLearning, which incorporated instructional design and computer programming. This certainly is not a great recipe for success, but it does demonstrate that we can come upon these things in many different ways.

Step 2: Creating Your Identity

This step came easy for me, although it did take time. I brainstormed several potential company names then scratched the majority of them off the list once I found that they already existed, as did their domains on the Web. Finally, I found one. I took immediate action and registered the domain, filed for a trademark, and was on my way. Interestingly, as I did my initial research I stumbled upon a company that was hiring contractors. That turned out to be my first (and current) client.

My next step in this process was to create an online presence. As I previously mentioned, I already secured the domain name. So, I created a meager Web site that would lay dormant for a long while. Again, not the best approach, but hey, I had to learn too.

Establishing a Web presence was only one of the six elements to this step. Creating a professional email account was accomplished when I selected a hosting provider for my Web site. For about the first year, I took only those only two actions toward creating my identity.

Next came professionalizing my phone line. I continue to use a mobile phone for business purposes. What I added was a professionally recorded voice mail. I paid $50 for my script to be recorded by a voice of my choice. The company I used for this had a lot of male and female options with online samples to review.

As you will read in my experience with Step 3 below, I had my Web pages professionally redesigned. A preparatory step was for a logo design. This only cost $49, and the vendor I selected came up with ten options from which to choose. Money well spent.

The remaining two elements of this step are social networking and advertising. Fully aware of the potential benefits to both of these elements, I still chose to disregard them. It was not until I hired an executive assistant (see Step 3 below) that I started to pay these areas any attention.

Step 3: Assembling Your Team and Network

For the better part of my first year as a software consultant, I worked alone without the need or desire for additional support. As the number of projects I was working on increased, certain areas of my business suffered. As is typical, the first thing to go was Web site maintenance. Also suffering were internal project ideas I designed but did not have time to develop.

My first team expansion was to contact a development team in the UK. They did great work for me with Web and CMS design and development. Not every developer is competent. I hired two different teams to develop two different Web sites. It was not long before I had to have the UK team fix the other team's site. Now, I only use the UK team for these types of projects. Once you find a good development team, keep them!

My second dip in these waters was to outsource a programming project I thoroughly designed, but did not have time to program. After receiving multiple bids on this project (all fixed price), I selected development team in India. I selected this team because they had evidence of previous related work and their bid was within my budget. They were not the lowest bidder, nor were they the highest.

At this point, I had two newly designed and published Web sites, thanks to a great team in the UK, and a team in India working on a project for me. As business kept picking up, those newly designed Web sites laid dormant. It was clear that I would never get to them, so I started the search for someone that could help. Like everything we talk about in this book, careful thought was required. I realized it was time for me to hire a full-time employee, and that is exactly what I did.

I hired an executive assistant that was computer savvy, was a professional blogger, and had an outgoing personality (the opposite of me). Executive assistants are wonderful assets especially if they are somewhat knowledgeable about your industry. My executive assistant performs the following functions for my company:

- Administrative organization
- Internet research
- Marketing
- Sales
- Web site maintenance
- Blog / news updates
- Software testing
- Demo / walk-thru development
- Content development
- External team coordination
- Keeps me on my toes

I know, you are reading that list and you do not believe one person can do all of that. Actually, I found one and you can too.

Step 4: Establishing Your Budget

If you read Case Study Part I you know that financial concerns were not at the forefront of my mind initially. Over time, I have made several hardware, software, reference, and other resource purchases. Detailing them here will not benefit you at all. What might be of interest is a list of my recurring costs. Because I have been able to capitalize on several free Internet-based services, my recurring costs are manageable. Some elements are listed without disclosing the specific cost for privacy purposes.

Expense	Cost	Frequency
EA Salary	*****	Monthly
Primary Internet Service	$ 59	Monthly
Secondary Internet Service	$ 60	Monthly
Business Phone Services	$ 124	Monthly
Various Online Data Backup Plans	$ 148	Yearly
Professional Organization Memberships	$ 375	Yearly
Professional Journals	$ 120	Yearly
Web Hosting	$ 134	Yearly
Office Supplies	$ 300	Yearly

Step 5: Developing a Pricing Model

My first experience with pricing models was with a fixed hourly rate. If the rate were for a short-term project like I suggested as an ideal situation in this chapter, it would have been a great experience. Instead, the project turned out to be a long-standing relationship with a client. Nearly two years into the contract, the rate has remained the same. This is an example of how not to do things.

After learning the important lesson of not signing on to an hourly rate for long projects or with repeat clients, I adopted a fixed price model for all other clients. Of course, to determine the fixed price, I have to use hourly calculations. My rates are based on the client and project. I have accepted many small projects at or below cost to beat out outsourcing to overseas options that are available to clients.

When I outsource work myself, or sub-contract, I never accept hourly rate bids. This is just too risky for me. I only accept fixed price bids or per-unit bids such as per-word price bids. Subcontractors want the work so they are happy to provide these types of bids.

Step 6: Marketing Yourself

Knowing what to do and actually doing it are two different things. I have seen the power of evangelizing your business through self-promotion or "marketing yourself." This is an area that I remain uncomfortable with and, as you might suspect, will likely prevent my business from rapid growth. That is a tradeoff I can live with. A steady business with slow growth is the right pace for me.

CHAPTER THREE

ALL ABOUT YOUR CLIENTS

Developing applications without a client is not an immediately profitable endeavor. Most people starting a software consultancy business have a refined skill set, one they want to share with paying clients. However, developing your own applications, without a client, is sure to keep your skills honed, even if it does not help pay the mortgage. Of course, it only takes one "killer app" to get your name out there and revenue streaming in. So, while you slowly work on that killer app, how about getting a few paying clients to help with that mortgage payment?

GETTING THEM

Acquiring new clients is an interesting part of this kind of business. There seems to be no single sure-fired method of getting new clients. Talk to twelve different software consultants about how they get clients, and you will receive a dozen different answers. What will be similar among their answers is that each will include one or more of the following methods:

1. Web site visitors
2. Repeat clients
3. Referrals
4. Responding to ads
5. Placing ads
6. Freelance marketplaces
7. Contract chasing
8. Develop and re-develop

Let's look at how the first six of these methods can help you acquire new clients. We will look at the last two methods when we discuss "Getting More of Them" in later in this chapter.

Web Site Visitors

How many people visit your Web site? How many of them contact you for services? How many of those that contact you become paying clients. Odds are you are not going to be happy with any of the answers to those questions, at least not in the beginning. Do the odds increase if you hire a Web designer, PR team, and pay for Search Engine Optimization (SEO)? Sure, but not by much. The Web is a sea of sites; yours will be just a single drop in that ocean. So, put some time and effort into designing your site and make it easy for visitors to contact you.

Maybe your outlook on this is, "If I acquire even one client via my Web site, then I will be happy." In this case, do not spend too much time and money on your site. If, however, you want your site to result in a constant and increasing flow of clients, then put the requisite effort into design, development, and maintenance of your site. Your level of effort and time is dependent upon what you want to get out of the site.

Repeat Clients

Having previous clients return to you for additional work is an ideal situation. If you do suitably impress the client with your knowledge, skills, attitudes, methods, affordability, and personality (yes, personality), then they are likely to return to you. When dealing with a new client you should conduct yourself in a manner that will result in them wanting to return to you for additional work.

Referrals

Not only do you want your clients to contact you when they have additional work, you want them to refer you to their friends, partners, and colleagues. You want clients to refer to you as, "my software guy," "my development team," or say "I have a guy for that." If they only think of you when it comes to their own consulting needs, they are likely to share your contact data, working methodologies, and costing model with their friends, partners, and colleagues.

Do not think that your hourly or specific job fees will not be revealed. How many times have you asked someone, "How much did you pay for that?" or "How much did that cost you?" Be consistent.

Responding to Ads

Companies that need work often advertise in periodicals and on Web sites that are appropriate for their industry or business. In some cases, they really just need to hire a software consultant instead of taking on a new employee. Contacting these companies about these ads could result in you earning a new contract.

Placing Ads

Should you spend money on marketing when you have not even landed your first paying gig? This might seem like putting the cart before the horse—it is. Sometimes this is necessary. It is possible to acquire clients to fill you up to work capacity without any advertising. This worked for me (see Case Study: Part III at the end of this chapter), but it might not work for everyone.

If you decide that you want to advertise, you need to determine what and where. The "what" part of this is the message or capability you want to express. Is your company name with a short bi-line enough? Do you need a flashy Web button? Public Relation firms are great at answering these questions. If you are serious about this, spend some of your business' seed money and hire a PR firm. They are not as expensive as you think.

The "where" to advertise question is a good one. There are so many options:

- Search engines
- Social networking sites
- Articles in eZines and magazines with your description and company information at the bottom
- Conference sponsorships
- News release service
- Pod casts
- Newspapers
- Trade journals / periodicals

These are just some of the options. The most important thing to remember is who your target audience is. Ensure your ad is appropriate for them and is placed in a medium that they are likely to see.

Freelance Marketplaces

Freelance marketplaces are online services for employers / individuals to find contract work. There are several of these services available and which one(s) you use (if you do at all) is a matter of preference. You can read about two of them in Chapter 4.

Employers use these services to find and vet freelancers for specific roles in specific projects. These are usually short-term contracts, but can extend to a few months. The employer posts a project description, required skills, location requirements (if any), budget (if known and willing to divulge), and time line. Freelancers can bid on these projects providing descriptive responses, cost, and ask clarifying questions. Employers are able to use the marketplace to review previous work, employer feedback, and online profiles for freelancers that bid on their project.

This is not a bad way to pick up small jobs and establish contact with employers around the globe. Bear in mind that these marketplaces are full of freelancers from several countries. The odds are that many of the freelancers have a cost of living much lower than what a U.S.-based software consultant has.

These services are excellent. Some marketplaces put the fees on the shoulders of the employer, while others put the burden on freelancers. Not all of these services are free, but many are.

KEEPING THEM

Clients are important commodities. Once you have one, you do not want to lose them. The keys to keeping a client are easy:

- Fair pricing
- Staying within time & cost projections
- Having clear and accessible communications
- Keeping the client involved and informed
- Delivering a superior product
- Providing continuing support

Let's look at each of these keys.

Fair Pricing

This should not have to be mentioned. A common mistake is to charge what you think you and your team's work is worth. Who can determine that? In Chapter 2, we talked about pricing models, so you should have an idea of how much it will cost you to perform the work. If your profit margin is too high, your clients are likely to find cheaper solutions to their future problems.

If you are having problems offering a fair price because you are paying your team high wages, it might be time to outsource some of your functions. This can result in a tremendous cost savings to you, lower prices for your clients, and more profit for you.

Staying within Time & Cost Projections

First, let's talk about staying within budget. If you and your client agree on a fixed price, you need to honor that. If additional functionality or components are requested after the contract is signed or the agreement is set, you can negotiate additional fees. Other than that circumstance, you should not be returning to the client looking for additional funds. If you incorrectly budgeted the project, you will learn the hard way how to prepare better budget projections in the future.

Depending upon how your contract is written or what you and your client agreed upon, your project might have very specific milestones. You will be involved with establishing these milestones and, in many cases, will develop them on your own. Once agreed upon, these milestones need to be met. When setting milestones, build in a little bit of time for unknown problems/difficulties. This will give you the opportunity to meet the milestones despite unforeseen circumstances and, in most cases, beat the milestone's deadline. So…under promise and over deliver.

Having Clear and Accessible Communications

Communication is more important than competency. You must be able to clearly communicate orally and in writing. How you speak and write has significant weight to how clients see you. They could form biases or wrong impressions of you based on your communication. Therefore, it is important to select a well-spoken and good writer to handle external communications.

When you bid on competitive projects, poorly written proposals can cause you not to be awarded the project. Knowing that articulation is important, it is advised that emails and other text documents be double checked before leaving your company.

Clarity in communications is not always how well something is written. It is equally important to speak clearly and at an even pace. Excitable mannerisms tend to make people nervous or uneasy. This is not what you want.

Accessibility of communications refers to making it easy for clients to talk with you. If they use an IM service that you do not, you should subscribe. Do not make your client bend to meet you. Rather, you need to flex to make it easy for them to communicate with you. There is a time issue as well. If you are on a different continent than your client, you should be prepared to work during their daylight hours. It is not usually necessary to adjust the working hours of your entire team, but the project manager, and you, should be readily available for meetings and to answer impromptu questions.

Keeping the Client Involved and Informed

Some of your clients will want to provide you with a specification document and/or have an initial virtual meeting with you, and then not want to talk to you until the project is completed. This is a recipe for disaster. Specification documents are rarely representative of 100 percent of the project. As features are developed, questions will come up, new ideas will emerge, and you will want to consult with the client throughout the process. Unless you are desperate for work, this is the kind of project to avoid.

Most clients will want some level of involvement. They might want project updates during weekly status meetings. Some will want to be involved in your internal team meetings. Each project is unique, so the ideal level of client involvement depends on several factors. There are a few things that you should keep in mind when setting up your client's expectations regarding their level of involvement. First, let them weigh-in on decisions before you go too far down a rabbit hole that might be wasted effort. Some clients enjoy being an observer on a design / development meeting. This gives them a sense of your competence. You can invite them to attend these meetings, but they are not likely to attend more than one if they are too technical. This is OK; you want them to know they are welcome and that you are not keeping anything from them. The bottom line here is to keep your client's comfort level high and to ensure they are involved as necessary to guarantee your team does not waste time and effort on features that are not needed.

Delivering a Superior Product

This goes without saying...I hope. Only take on projects on which you are confident you can hit a home run. If you are awarded a project, for example, that requires a server-side database and embedded IM feature, but are only well-versed in one of those areas, your end product might not be "superior." Of course, this does not mean you should always pass on projects for which you will have to develop new capacities, rather, only bid on projects that you know you can deliver a great product. Taking on projects where you have to develop new capacities is a great way to expand your business.

Providing Continuing Support

It can be argued that product support is more important than the product itself. Look at the PC hardware industry. There are a lot of companies that build PCs on demand and from a global component inventory system. This can result in virtually the same physical computer from many different "manufacturers." What makes one company better than the other? Their customer service and product support. In the early 1990s, when computer hardware companies were popping up all over the place, the reviews always seemed to focus on their customer service and product support.

It is not uncommon to offer a specific period of time where you will provide product support as part of the contract. If there are bugs in your software, you should feel obligated to fix them anyway. Beyond that fixed period, usually twelve months, additional support should be billable. This is something you establish in your contract.

GETTING MORE OF THEM

At this point, you have a small list of clients and you have done all the right things to keep them coming back to you when they have additional work. The problem is it could be several years in between projects for a particular client. That does not result in steady work, so you need more clients.

In addition to the techniques we talked about in the "Getting Them" section earlier in this chapter, here are tactics that could increase your client pool.

Contract Chasing

Reading trade publications, professional blogs, and eZines is a great way to stay on top of your industry and, more importantly, the industry from which you want clients. For example, if you are in the software development industry, you will follow a set of related publications, blogs, and eZines. If your niche is developing for education, then you should follow education-related digital and print material. The media often covers large contract awards.

There are a lot of companies that bid on large projects, and then grow their company to meet the need. This means if you see company ABC earning a huge governmental contract, it is likely that company ABC will be looking to quickly grow their internal capabilities. This usually means a bunch of contract work and short-term employees. Contacting company ABC with information of your capabilities and interest in their new project could land you a lucrative contract.

Unlike ambulance chasing, there is no shame in this tactic.

Develop and Re-Develop

If you have the time and resources, you can develop or partially develop a "software solution" to post on your Web site. The purpose of this application is to show potential clients what you are capable of and how it can be customized for them. I call this develop and re-develop. You essentially create a shell of an application then modify it for specific clients. This is a costly approach, but one that could pay huge dividends for you.

Case Study: Part III

Our case study continues. In Part III, I detail my approach to clients, including how I acquire them and how I keep them coming back for more. This chapter presented several approaches and tactics regarding client acquisition. This is serious business, without clients, you will go out of business. Our case study details my approach, which, it is important to remember, works for me, but might not be the ideal approach for you. Digest this chapter's content and map out your own approach, one that you are comfortable with and that works for you.

Getting Them

As you will recall, there were eight components to getting new clients presented in this chapter. The first was Web site visitors. My Web approach was to develop a site that I could drive people to during the bidding process. If someone stumbled upon my site and contacted me, that would be great, but not my expectation. This approach protected me from false expectations. I did not believe the adage, "if you build it, they will come." There is too much competition and Web-noise for me to put too much hope into getting lucky. This being said, I did develop my sites sufficiently to project a professional image, give insights into my capabilities, link to works completed, and make it easy to contact me.

The second "Getting Them" component mentioned in this chapter, repeat clients, is where I put my the majority of my energy. My first client hired me as an instructional designer for a two-year project. As the project progressed, their team needed additional services. It was not long before additional capabilities of mine came into focus. This turned me into a multi-faceted prime asset for several different projects. If I were only to bid on projects that used my full skill set, I am sure I would be working in a fast food chain to pay my mortgage. Instead, it is OK to bid on projects that only use one or two of your skills. These limited jobs can often turn into repeat clients.

I discovered, via a tech-podcast, the world of freelancer marketplaces a year after staring my business. If I had known about them in the beginning, life would have been much easier earlier. Of course, if a book like the one you are reading now were available to me, learning about freelancer marketplaces would have been well worth the purchase price. I use two freelancer marketplaces; both are featured in Chapter 4. I use one as an employer when I need work done that is outside my team's skill set, or that we do not have time to do. The other, I use to bid on open projects. This has worked very well for me. I only bid on projects that I am interested in, have the capability to complete, and think I would be a good fit for. I have to pass on a lot of projects, because there are so many of them and I do not have the capacity to do them all. This is good news for new consultants—there is a lot of work out there.

The develop and re-develop approach is something I firmly believe in, although I have had limited success with it. The biggest detractor is that developing a software solution without a paying client takes time away from you and your team, time that could be spent on paying projects. As time permits, energy can be spent on these types of projects.

The remaining components of getting new clients are referrals, responding to ads, placing ads, and contract chasing. Other than referrals, I have opted to stay away from placing or responding to ads and contract chasing. There really is not enough time, unless you have a full-time business development person, to adopt all of these approaches at once.

Keeping Them

In this chapter, we talked about fair pricing, staying within time/cost projections, clear and accessible communications, keeping the client involved/informed, delivering a superior product, and providing continuing support. Unlike establishing an approach to getting clients, you cannot mix and match the "Keeping Them" strategies. Details of how I handle each one is provided on the next couple of pages.

Fair Pricing

For some jobs, I bid below what I would normally charge for a job. Sometimes it is more important to get a couple of projects under your belt than to earn quick money. How can you develop your portfolio if you are too selective? This was my concern, so I underbid on a couple of projects that did not take much time or effort. This has the dual benefit of enhancing my portfolio and growing my client pool. It is always a hope that they will come back for additional work. For larger projects, I set my rates at a reasonable level. This is possible due to low overhead (see the budget section of Case Study II for details).

Staying within Time & Cost Projections

These are really two issues, both of which are important to the client. Whenever I bid on a project, it is based on a development and production cycle. I use Gantt charts to provide a visible representation of the schedule. I make it very clear that my prototype iterations are tied to timely feedback from the client. If the time slips, it must be at the client's request. Building in a small time cushion helps. For cost projections, I have the policy of never going back to the client for additional monies. If my planning was incorrect, I should bear the additional cost, not the client. In cases when the client asks for components that are not in the original design specification, I negotiate a fee for it. Doing so prevents scope creep without compensation.

Having Clear and Accessible Communications / Keeping the Client Involved and Informed

There is a balance between communicating with a client too much and not communicating with a client enough. The solution is based on the project and your client. For short projects, there really is no time to "figure out" what your client wants. Therefore, it is best to talk about this. What I have done for short projects is to tell clients what I am working on for the current iteration before it starts. This gives them the opportunity to weigh-in on my plans. So, when I release a new prototype, I tell them what is in it, and what is planned for the next round. With a rapid development cycle of one to two weeks, this seems to provide ample communication between my clients and my team.

For larger projects, I use, depending on the client, a bulletin board software system or online project management system. There is a plethora of this software available free as well as some pretty nifty premium ones. I learned early on that not all clients want to use one of these systems. Some prefer email while others like IM or phone conversations. Being flexible is the key.

Delivering a Superior Product

Nothing needs to be said here other than every product I deliver has my name on it. Each product can lead to additional work or prevent you from getting additional work. Taking pride in your work is important. I subscribe to the theory that our work represents our capabilities and us.

Providing Continuing Support

I always include twelve months of free bug fixes. If I created software with a lot of bugs, then this would not be to my benefit. Delivering a superior product takes care of this. I have yet to be called upon to fix a bug. It has been said that no software is bug-free. It has also been said that bugs are just undocumented features.

Chapter Four

Collaboration and Management Tools

Every job uses tools. Carpenters use hammers and saws; chefs use knives and strainers; and referees use whistles. What about software consultants? Our tools can be categorized into hardware and software. Let's leave the hardware category alone so readers are not separated into Mac and PC camps. Both platforms, by the way, will serve you well. I use both.

There are more software tools than there are trees in the rain forest. How then do we decide which tools to use? The answer to that is usually a mix of user preference and trial and error. There is no perfect set of tools; you probably already have a set that you like and will continue to use. The tools described below are the ones I use the most. Some are free and some cost money. They all are worth more than they charge. Think about how much each tool benefits your business, how much more efficient it makes you and your team, and how much money you would have to spend to develop your own tool. With that in mind, these tools are all well underpriced.

Categorizing software tools is difficult because so many of them can be used for multiple purposes. Nevertheless, the software tools featured here have been organized into five primary categories.

1. Time management & coordination
2. Communications & Web conferencing
3. Data organization & management
4. Image / audio / video tools
5. Freelance marketplaces

Each tool will be covered within its primary category in the following format:

- Name of tool
- What it is / What it does
- Cost / pricing model
- Where you can get it
- Tool attribution
- Case study

This chapter is different from the preceding and remaining chapters in that the case study is provided in the main chapter—as part of each tool description. OK, let's talk about the "Sweet Sixteen Tools" (in no particular order).

TIME MANAGEMENT & COORDINATION TOOLS

Toggl

What it is / What it does: Toggl is a time tracking software application / service. It works within an Internet browser, on your desktop (PC, Mac, and Linux), and on your intranet. It has a load of features but is easy to use. It includes customizable views, branding, multiple users, and an amazing reporting module. You can organize your work by project, client, and task.

Cost / Pricing Model: free and premium options

Where you can get it: http://www.toggl.com

Tool Attribution: Apprise (http://www.apprise.eu)

Case Study: I listed this tool first because I wish I knew about it when I first started. When it was time for me to hire my first full-time employee, I scoured the Web for time tracking software and did not find anything I thought would suit my needs. I finally decided to develop my own application and turned back to the Web to look for inspiration. That is when I found Toggl. I knew I could not develop anything as good as what they had done, and started to experiment with their software. It took me about two minutes to become a fan of Toggl. I now use Toggle everyday to track my time and that of my executive assistant. Here are some of the other things I use Toggl for:

- Compiling time-based invoices
- Tracking project-specific and task-specific time expenditures
- Projecting time for future projects based on past projects

Doodle

What it is / What it does: Doodle is an amazing online scheduling tool. It makes scheduling events with distributed teams extraordinarily easy. You can create a poll with dates and times and invite your team members to indicate which dates and times work for them and which ones do not. Times can be displayed as local time for each poll member. To make it even easier, Doodle provides the administrator with email notifications when users submit their input. Seeing is believing; you really owe it to yourself and your business to give this tool a try.

Cost / Pricing Model: free and premium options

Where you can get it: http://www.doodle.com

Tool Attribution: Doodle AG

Case Study: In my time as a software consultant, I have yet to work with anyone in the same state (U.S.). In fact, I deal with more people on other continents than I do my own. Scheduling meetings with distributed teams can be full of confusion and missed opportunities. Doodle to the rescue. Trust me, once you try Doodle, you will bookmark their site!

Bonus: The Doodle AG team is giving a free 1-year premium Doodle subscription to the first fifty readers that use the coupon code bd7vxbb3. The coupon is can be used at: http://doodle.com/premium. Log in today to see if there are any subscriptions left.

Meeting Ticker

What it is / What it does: This amazingly simple but useful tool keeps track of how much your meeting costs. Type in the number of attendees, their average hourly wage, the time the meeting started, and click "start." The user is then presented with a money counter that is updated every second. This fun application supports four different currencies.

Cost / Pricing Model: free to use

Where you can get it: http://tobytripp.github.com/meeting-ticker.com

Tool Attribution: Written by Toby Tripp, Lydia Tripp, and Roy Kolak

Case Study: Have you ever been in a meeting where conversation drifted from the agenda? Well, I have. When you are in control of these meetings, you can use the Meeting Ticker to keep track of how much money is being spent (or wasted). I once suggested that a client use this tool in a meeting where there were seven different subcontractors—costs add up fast.

COMMUNICATIONS & WEB CONFERENCING TOOLS

Skype

What it is / What it does: By now, I doubt there are many Internet users that are not aware of Skype. Their well-known stature is due to their incredible software and service. Skype represents a full suite of communication services that include free skype-to-skype calls, calls to landlines/mobile phones, text messaging, voicemail, and video conferencing. Their list of services is incredible and can be found at http://skype.com/allfeatures. One of the greatest things about Skype is that it is a cross-platform application working on Macs, PCs, and Linux machines.

Cost / Pricing Model: free, pay-as-you-go, and monthly plans

Where you can get it: http://www.skype.com

Tool Attribution: Skype Limited

Case Study: Skype is one of the tools I use every day without fail. The Skype features I use most frequently are instant messaging and audio / video conferencing. When I travel overseas, I subscribe to a plan that includes unlimited calls to landlines. I would rather give my money to Skype than the hotel. I also purchased one of their headsets and it works famously.

Adium

What it is / What it does: Adium is an instant messaging system that runs on Macs. This is not another IM client; it connects you to over a dozen IM clients. You can connect to all your IM accounts in one application. Amazing, I know. For a similar application for the PC, see Trillian Atra by Cerulean Studios at http://www.trillian.im.

Cost / Pricing Model: free / open source (donations accepted)

Where you can get it: http://www.adium.im

Tool Attribution: Adium was completely developed by volunteers. There is no corporation behind Adium, just a bunch of brilliant folks willing to dedicate their free time and talent.

Case Study: I am probably like most people that spend their lives in front of a computer in that I have multiple IM accounts. I have one for personal use, one for academic use, and one for business use. The latest version of Adium is always up and running on my computer. If I am doing work for a client, I will have Adium connect to the IM account that I use for work; if I am doing work for the University, I will enable the IM account I put on my syllabi; and if I am not busy in one of those two roles, I will enable my personal IM account. One of the great things about Adium is that it is easy to connect and disconnect to individual and multiple IM accounts. This is much better than having to monitor multiple IM clients all in separate applications.

Dimdim

What it is / What it does: Dimdim is a relatively new Web conferencing / live Webinar service. What makes Dimdim unique? One of their best features is the fact that there is no software installation required. The software runs completely within a browser. That makes Dimdim a truly cross-platform solution. Other features include screen sharing, Web page sharing, conferencing with audio and/or video, presentation of PowerPoint and PDFs, robust chat, whiteboard, and the ability to record meetings.

Cost / Pricing Model: free to use, premium subscriptions required for meetings larger than twenty people

Where you can get it: http://www.dimdim.com

Tool Attribution: Dimdim Inc.

Case Study: I use Dimdim for a weekly meeting where we take turns sharing our screens. Dimdim is so easy to use that my newest employee ran her first meeting with us via Dimdim. One of the features we really like is the ability to set up meetings in advance and send email notifications to participants. The email, generated by Dimdim, includes a hyperlink to the meeting.

GoToMeeting

What it is / What it does: GoToMeeting is one of the powerhouses of Web conferencing. It is feature rich, allowing meeting participants the ability to share and pause screen sharing, promote attendees as presenters, and chat privately and publicly. GoToMeeting supports both Macs and PCs and requires a minimal local install. You can set up your meetings in advance and have email notifications sent to all participants. There is also the option to use audio via call-in.

Cost / Pricing Model: moderate monthly fee for unlimited meetings, significant savings for those signing up for an annual contract

Where you can get it: http://www.gotomeeting.com

Tool Attribution: Citrix Online, LLC

Case Study: Although I do not subscribe to GoToMeeting, I use them weekly with a longstanding client. GoToMeeting has never failed in the nearly two years that I have used the service. It is great to be able to set up several meetings in advance, each being assigned their own meeting URL. Also, the ability to pause screen sharing is nice. In addition, I have attended a few Webinars that were hosted by GoToMeeting. These were equally flawless. If you are going to have frequent meetings, this is worth looking into. You can sign up for a free thirty-day trial.

eFax

What it is / What it does: Want to send and receive faxes on-line without a fax machine? eFax is the answer. They provide you with a fax number that you can distribute to your clients, enabling you to receive emails via email regardless if you are near your fax machine. This may be the final straw for landlines; do we really need them anymore? Depending upon which service you sign up for, you can select your phone number and receive your voicemail as an audio file attached to your email.

Cost / Pricing Model: free and premium subscriptions

Where you can get it: www.efax.com

Tool Attribution: j2 Global Communications, Inc.

Case Study: I moved from a traditional fax machine to eFax the first time I was expecting a fax and was on travel. I have never switched back.

DATA ORGANIZATION & MANAGEMENT TOOLS

Google Docs

What it is / What it does: Google Docs is another free and incredible online software suite from Google. You can create, share, and collaborate asynchronously as well as in real time. Document types supported are word processing documents, spreadsheets, and presentations. There are so many features; they cannot be adequately covered in this chapter. Go to http://www.google.com/google-d-s/tour1.html to take a virtual tour of the service. Here are features that are just too good not to mention:

- Online, safe storage
- Organize files in folders
- Set individual or folder-level sharing controls
- Invite people to collaborate or view your documents
- Upload existing files in several different formats
- Send files via email to your Google Docs account

Google provides a lot of very professional templates to use. Of course, you can start documents from scratch as well. There are also user-provided templates to get you started.

Cost / Pricing Model: free, free, free

Where you can get it: http://docs.google.com

Tool Attribution: Google

Case Study: My office is a virtual one, my team is distributed, and I do not have a company intranet. With Google Docs, I am able to store files securely that I want to share. I organize the files by project, which makes navigating the folder structure easy. I routinely scan the document listing to see if any of them were updated.

Evernote

What it is / What it does: Evernote is an ingenious information storage system. You install the software on your Mac and/or PC and set up notebooks to organize your information. The information inside each notebook is called a note. Notes can come from a variety of sources: you can simply type text; you can drag and drop a file; take a screen shot; use your Web camera to record a note; copy and paste a note, or import a file. The interface is slick and easy to use. As would be expected, the interfaces are different on Macs and PCs, but they both work brilliantly. Evernote even works on some mobile phones.

Finding your information is extremely easy. You can tag your notes to support tag searches, search by keywords, search by title, or use browsing tools. An amazing feature is that text inside images is also searchable.

OK, now for the really amazing feature. The software you install on your computer synchs with your online account. That means that you can work remotely and still have access to all your data. You can also work offline then synch your account the next time your computer connects to the Internet. Synching is automatic, but you can also manually synch your information.

Cost / Pricing Model: free and premium subscriptions

Where you can get it: http://www.evernote.com

Tool Attribution: Evernote Corporation

Case Study: Evernote is a tool that I use every day. I have a premium subscription, which gives me a tremendous monthly upload allowance and unlimited file synchronization types. One of the things I use Evernote for is to share files and information easily between my Macs and PC. I also use the notes feature to record fleeting thoughts and capture Web information for later consumption. My computers have rigorous backup systems, but all local. Instead of investing in cloud storage, I use Evernote. In addition, I used Evernote to type this book. Writing a book takes a tremendous amount of time and effort; I did not want to take even the slightest chance that my work would be lost.

dotProject

What it is / What it does: dotProject is an open source project management tool. This software requires a MySQL database, so you will want to install it on one of your servers. It is a complex tool, so it is not as intuitive as you would like. It only takes a short while to become accustomed to the system and become efficient in its use. The hierarchy of the information is companies --> projects --> tasks. The task information is very robust, including progress percentage, human resource allocations, notes, start/stop dates, and target budget. There are some great management tools such as calendar view, email notifications, Gantt charts, task logs, and forums.

Cost / Pricing Model: free open source project; managed and supported by a group of volunteers and a strong user base

Where you can get it: http://www.dotproject.net

Tool Attribution: dotProject was completely developed by volunteers. There is no corporation behind dotProject, just a bunch of brilliant folks willing to dedicate their free time and talent.

Case Study: dotProject is at the core of my workflow management. Each project is entered into the system with tasks and milestones. These tasks are assigned to specific employees or teams and, as applicable, subordinated to other tasks. As tasks are completed or progress is made on them, employees update the task by logging information (easy to do). This results in my ability to view a project and monitor the progress at a glance. There is a bit of time overhead associated with setting dotProject up, but it is well worth the time.

IMAGE / AUDIO / VIDEO TOOLS

Balsamiq Mockups

What it is / What it does: Balsamiq Mockups is an extremely easy to use, but powerful screen mockup software application. I hasten to say it is a "screen" mockup application, because it can be used to mockup entire systems. The creators made this application so easy to use that you will be creating mockups as soon as the application opens. At the heart of its functionality is the ability to create graphical user interfaces for software that you are currently designing. This is a great way to generate screen mockups with standard interface objects (it comes with seventy-five) quickly. Showing these mockups to clients helps in two ways. First, you save a lot of time by using Mockups instead of programming sample interfaces. Secondly, you can get GUI samples to your clients in record time.

This software tool is amazing. If you are involved in system design, GUI design, programming, or client relations, you are going to want to review this software. This brief section only covered a few of the benefits of using Mockups and its features. There is a great three-minute video on the product home page (see URL below) that will give you a great introduction to the product.

Cost / Pricing Model: trial version with reasonable individual licensing (multiple installs)

Where you can get it: http://www.balsamiq.com/products/mockups

Tool Attribution: Balsamiq SRL / Balsamiq Studios, LLC

Case Study: I do a lot of custom software development and have integrated the use of Balsamiq Mockups into my design process. Once all the features and specifications are obtained from the client, we perform a data structure and feature organization analysis to help lay a foundation for future development work. Following this analysis, we use Balsamiq Mockups to provide the client with a few options for their GUI. What works really well is to send them a couple of screen shots before the meeting, each numbered sequentially. During the meeting, we discuss with the client what they like / dislike about each of the samples. Clients really enjoy participating in a Web conference where I can make immediate changes to a GUI in Balsamiq Mockups. I share my screen during this process and it is always a great experience for the client. This also makes the GUI design process much quicker and efficient. After the Web conference, we can start programming the UI, assured that we are programming what the client wants.

Bonus: The Balsamiq Studios team has offered a discount to anyone reading this book. At checkout, just enter the coupon code: FRLCUN. The price of the software is already inexpensive, but I hope this generous coupon will give you a reason to check out Balsamiq Mockups. It will change your business!

Skitch

What it is / What it does: Skitch is a screen capture software application that is bundled with amazing features. This Mac-only application allows you to snap your desktop, a specific window, or any screen section. Selection is made via crosshairs, your Web camera, or a framed window. There is even a time-delay capture feature, which is very handy. Once you snapped the image, there is a host of options available to you. You can resize, annotate, save, color, flip, rotate, shadow, and the list goes on. An online component to Skitch allows you easily to share your skitches.

Cost / Pricing Model: one time, reasonably priced purchase

Where you can get it: http://skitch.com

Tool Attribution: Plasq (http://plasq.com)

Case Study: Skitch has become one of the core tools of my business. Here are a few things I routinely use Skitch for:

- Capture screens during Web conferences and webinars
- Snap images from objects I create in presentation software
- Create system guides / user guides with screenshots
- Snap system images and drag them from Skitch to my IM software during IM chats
- Easily resize images to specific height / width dimensions

In addition, I use Skitch's history feature, which makes it very easy to snap, save, and forget. Well, not forget. You can easily go back to the graphical history to retrieve your saved skitches.

ScreenFlow

What it is / What it does: ScreenFlow is a professional screen-casting software application. You can capture your entire desktop as well as audio from your microphone and speakers. This application makes it very easy to produce professional screencasts. Once your recording is completed, you have incredible editing tools at your disposal, which includes the ability to crop the screen. Additional features include picture-in-picture, motion effects, callouts, customizable cursors, color correction, audio editing, auto-attenuation, time-lapse, freeze frame, and transitions.

ScreenFlow supports export to multiple formats with high quality results. You can export an entire screencast or selected segments. Their latest version supports direct export to YouTube.

Cost / Pricing Model: one time, reasonably priced purchase

Where you can get it: http://www.telestream.net/screenflow

Tool Attribution: Telestream, Inc.

Case Study: ScreenFlow is my application of choice when recording software demonstration videos and video walk-throughs.

FREELANCE MARKETPLACES

Guru

What it is / What it does: Guru.com is a Web service that connects employers with freelancers. The marketplace' over one million registered users are divided into employers and freelancers.

For employers, Guru.com represents an excellent method of finding immediate, short- or long- term freelance help for your projects. You can search the freelance directory or create a project for freelancers to bid on. Project creation is very easy with Guru.com. Here are the primary data elements you can enter for each project:

- Basic Information
  - ☐ Project title
  - ☐ Description
  - ☐ Estimated budget
- Skill Requirements
  - ☐ Primary skill (e.g., flash & Web animation)
  - ☐ Secondary skills (e.g., graphic design)
  - ☐ Industry experience
- Location specification
- Project type (public or private)
- Additional information
  - ☐ Onsite / offsite
  - ☐ Bidding duration
- Questions for freelancers

Attachments can be included in project postings. Typical attachments include design specifications and screenshots. In the employer role, it is best if you keep your projects open for the entire bidding window you specify. This gives all freelancers a fair shot at bidding on your project, and not just the first bidders.

Depending upon your project, you could receive more bids than you have time to review. This is a nice problem to have.

For freelancers, Guru.com is a wonderful service. First, freelancers create a profile that will be available to potential employers. These profiles can consist of:

- Overview
  - Name, motto, logo, rating
- Summary information
  - Location
  - Earnings history (all time and last twelve months)
  - Rate
  - Skill categories
  - Industry(ies)
- Highlights
  - Textual information about your services, methods, etc.
- Skills
  - Years of experience
  - Highest degree earned
  - Software skills
  - Additional skills
  - Tested skills
- Work terms
- Images / videos
- Company information
- Work samples
- Completed projects

Once a freelancer establishes a profile, s/he can search projects and bid on them. Also, new projects, meeting specific criteria, are delivered to the freelancer's email inbox. Submitting a proposal is a very easy process that includes a total estimated cost, a written proposal, and questions for the employer. Discussion threads are supported between the employer and freelancer.

Guru.com supports the project through completion, including escrow, invoicing, payments, and even arbitration.

Cost / Pricing Model: small transaction fees

Where you can get it: http://www.guru.com

Tool Attribution: Guru.com

Case Study: Guru.com has been my magic elixir. I use the service as both an employer and a freelancer. I only bid on projects that I am capable of fulfilling and ones that are interesting or for social good (e.g., educational games, social awareness, etc.). The majority of my clients have originated from a Guru.com project.

Elance

What it is / What it does: Elance is a Web service that connects employers with freelancers. It is a marketplace with over 60,000 employers and over 90,000 freelancers. These employers include small, mid-range, and large companies. There are significant financial benefits to outsourcing projects or components of projects to freelancers. Jobs are identified by the below listed categories, then subdivided by skills in demand.

- Web & programming
- Design & multimedia
- Writing & translation
- Administrative support
- Sales & marketing
- Finance & management
- Legal
- Engineering & manufacturing

Users can act as an employer and freelancer with just one account. This is a very convenient feature. Financial transactions at Elance are easy, flexible, and safe.

Cost / Pricing Model: small transaction fees

Where you can get it: http://www.elance.com

Tool Attribution: Elance, Inc.

Case Study: My use of Elance has been to acquire translation and voice over services. Creating a project on Elance was intuitive and the management of that project was easy.

FINAL NOTE ON TOOLS

The "Sweet Sixteen Tools" covered in this chapter are the ones I use the most and strongly encourage new and current software consultants to review. None of these are paid advertisements for products. I did contact each company to ensure my information was accurate and to seek publication permission. In a couple of cases, the companies even provided a coupon code to give you, the reader—a discount on their software / service.

CASE STUDY: PART IV

In addition to using this chapter's referenced software tools and services, I use commercial software for professional documents (Microsoft Office by the Microsoft Corporation and iWork by Apple Inc.), accounting (QuickBooks by Intuit, Inc.), and personal task management (Remember the Milk by Remember the Milk). Even with this full suite of software, there are tools that I have had to develop in-house to support my consulting business.

Time Watcher

My consulting business is comprised of team members geographically separated. Managing a distributed team is made much easier when using the tools in this chapter. The element of time is always an issue. I used to find myself typing, "time in Manila," or "time in Perth" consistently into Google's search bar to determine what time it was in locations where my team members and clients were located. From this repetitive act, came the idea for Time Watcher. It is a simple application that provides tremendous functionality. It has six digital clocks, one for the local time and five others for selectable time zones/cities. We added clock labels so we could go behind just seeing the city's name.

If you want to see the tool in action, go to this URL:

http://www.three19.com/timewatcher

Project Information Portal (Pip)

Bulletin boards and dry erase boards in conference rooms provide a great opportunity for team communications. Virtual teams do not have this luxury. My consulting firm almost always has several active projects and did not have a dry erase board where the entire team could glance at it for a quick status update on each project. That is where we came up with the idea for a Project Information Portal (or Pip for short). Pip is an application we developed in-house that runs on Macs, PCs, and in a browser. Pip has a tabbed interface, each pulling specific data from our servers or other online information. The tabs, which are indicative of Pip's design, are White Board, Quick Links, Time Watcher, Note Manager, and system. Also, an ever-present notes widget displays incoming notes from other Pip users.

If you want to see screenshots of the tool, go to this URL:

http://www.idleaders.com/pip

Collaborative Agile Production (CAP) Software

We use an agile approach to software development with many scrum methodologies. We developed CAP as an electronic collaborative software application (ECSA) to support non-collocated teams in the agile/scrum process. CAP can be used asynchronously or synchronously. CAP system information is stored in a server-side database for quick retrieval and easy backups.

CAP features a virtual white board set up in true agile/scrum fashion with columns for: Product Backlog, Task To Do, Work

In Progress, To Be Verified, and Done. There is an instant chat system for synchronous communications. A status bar keeps the user aware of the current project, the last update, who is editing, and who is viewing. Control of the board can be relinquished to viewers, thereby promoting them to editor.

On CAP's virtual white board is an unlimited amount of customizable notes that can move from column to column as your project progresses. There is also a full set of customizable system settings, including frequency of updates, font size/color, and color/size/shape of the notes. Other features include:

- Authenticated user access
- Remote access
- Multi-user support
- Multiple-project support
- Full customization
- Auto-save / auto-refresh
- Robust help system

If you want to learn more about this tool, go to this URL:

http://www.three19.com/cap

CHAPTER FIVE

SOFTWARE DEVELOPMENT

A chapter on software development in a software consulting book? You might be thinking that software development is a topic best suited for textbooks, and you could be right. We will discuss software development as it applies to software consulting, specifically how to manage the process with your client in mind.

YOUR CORE COMPETENCY

One of the prerequisites to starting a successful software consulting firm is to have software design and/or development as your core competency. In today's global business world, almost everything can be outsourced, so you need to have something that others do not, or at least be very good at your firm's core functions. You should be prepared to answer the question, "What is your company's core competency?" It is recommended that you take the time to think this though. Once you have firmly established what your core competency is, you should focus on that, and even improve upon it.

So what is a core competency? Can you have more than one of them? Core competencies are the things your firm does best that benefit your clients. Your core competency could be that you have a team of speech therapists that have unique research. Your firm leverages this research to create age-targeted language training. Another example is that you have an advance team of Ruby on Rails developers. In this example, you leverage your talent pool to develop cutting edge technologies and software solutions.

Identifying, embracing, and enhancing your firm's core competencies is critical to ensure your competitiveness.

PROGRAMMING LANGUAGE / PLATFORM DECISIONS

Clients drive requirements. These requirements might be stated simply as "Convert this board game into a computer game for the Internet." Non-tech savvy clients are usually vague, which is OK. They do not need to be tech-savvy—they have you. Other clients might provide you with a very detailed design specification, which includes the requirement to develop in a specific programming language and even provide the version number. This can be disconcerting. It is advisable to consider which programming language is best suited for the job. The language your team is the most proficient in is not always the best solution, nor is the one your client demands always the best choice.

In cases when a client selects the language, it is best to talk with them about their reasoning. Sometimes they include the language because they think they know which language is best suited for the project. Other times they select a language because they have in-house personnel that are somewhat proficient in that language. Their hope is that future modifications/upgrades can be done in-house, thereby saving them money. Talking with your client about the language they selected will reveal their reasoning and give you an opportunity to provide them with alternatives, should you feel it necessary.

The "platform decision" refers to which operating systems / hardware platforms you will be developing for use. This can be expressed as Mac or PC, Mac OS, Linux, a specific Windows version, Mobile Phones, Web application, an application for a social networking site, or even a game console. Clients usually have a firm understanding of what their platform requirements are. This is sometimes an area where you can provide clients with something in addition to what they request, without additional cost to them. If they ask for a PC application, why not deliver versions for the PC, Mac, and the Web? If they ask for a Web-based application, why not offer them Mac and PC versions as well, without additional cost? How can you do that? Depending on your programming language choice, developing programs for the Mac, PC, Linux, and the Web could be as easy as developing for just one platform. If you are not a believer, you will be when you read the next section, A Revolutionary Approach.

A Revolutionary Approach

You made it through four and a half chapters and are now to be rewarded with the revelation of what the book's by-line, "A Revolutionary Approach," is all about.

There is a company in Edinburgh, Scotland called Runtime Revolution Ltd. that produces Revolution, a flexible, powerful, and easy to use, software development environment. Those three adjectives are seldom used to describe the same thing. In this case, it is warranted. At the core of the development environment is the revTalk programming language, which has an English-like syntax. The language is very easy to learn whether or not you already know one or more programming languages.

Benefits of using this programming language include:

- Decreased development time
- Increases productivity
- Easier software maintenance
- Ability to develop for Mac, PC, Linux, and the Web

There is a very strong, supportive, and active user base that is quick to help on revTalk forums and listservs. The user base includes software professionals, academics, and enthusiasts. The level of feedback and support provided by the user base is amazing as is the speed in which calls for help are answered.

There are several product types that use revTalk:

- revMedia · for beginning programmers and academia
- revStudio · for commercial and business
- revEnterprise · an enterprise-level package

revMedia is free to everyone. It is not a trial or demo version, it is truly free. You can learn more about revMedia and download it at http://revmedia.runrev.com/revMedia.

There is even a server-side scripting language called iRev. To learn more about any of the RunRev products, visit http://www.runrev.com.

At the end of this chapter, we will continue our case study. There you will learn how I use revTalk to power my business.

THE DESIGN AND DEVELOPMENT PROCESS

Talk to twenty software developers and they will describe their design and development processes, each one different from the others. How you design and develop software is for you to decide; there is no single best method. Your processes will depend upon your team, the projects, and your timeline. It is important to have an internal set of design and development processes documented, trained to, and utilized. This sets a certain level of operating standards within your firm and allows for teams to function more efficiently and for teams to work more autonomously.

There are traditional methods such as the waterfall methodology, which includes a series of regimented, sequential steps.

These steps typically include requirements, design, implementation, verification, and maintenance. This traditional approach has been branded as inefficient because its lack of process feedback during the process.

The spiral methodology has four quadrants of analysis, evaluation, development, and planning. Each of these quadrants is addressed as the process spirals through them. This is an iterative approach to software design and development, but without refined phases.

Software prototyping is sometimes referred to as a design and development methodology, but really should be a preliminary step in most design processes.

There are a lot of other methodologies, including agile/scrum, extreme programming, rapid application development, unified process, top-down programming, and incremental. Which design methodology you use is not important. What is important is that you define your processes and institute some level of flexibility to account for the unknown variables of project specifics and client desires.

CASE STUDY: PART V

Core Competencies

Deciding on a core competency for my business was something I initially thought I had a good handle on. I started as an Instructional Designer, with a fresh ID graduate degree. It was not long before I started moving toward my natural desire to program. Previous undergraduate and graduate degrees prepared me well for a career in programming or information systems management. Not wanting to give one area up for the other, I decided to merge the two areas of interest. My core competency became educational game programming. That is not to say I only do that kind of work, but it is my firm's area of focus, or core competency.

As stated earlier in this chapter, we should continually develop our core competencies. I accomplish this by reading industry periodicals, professional and academic journals, and subscribing to blogs, podcasts, and listservs. My adjunct teaching jobs also require me to stay current.

Platform Decisions / Programming Language

My firm's expertise lies with desktop software application development. We develop for the Mac and PC. If a client will resell their product, we always offer both Mac and PC versions even if they only ask for one. When they learn they can get both versions without any additional cost, they are very happy. We accomplish this by using Revolution. Developing for more than one platform in Revolution is just the matter of a single check box. It is unbelievably easy.

My team has the combined expertise of several different programming languages and I even teach Java at a local university and C++ at a local community college. Even with experience in advanced and mainstream programming languages, revTalk is my first choice. I am usually able to provide my clients with the first prototype of their application in two to three days. If the program is extremely in-depth and complicated, I still endeavor to deliver an early prototype in two to three days. These prototypes do not always have full functionality and they never have final graphics. Delivering a prototype that fast is a sure way to endear clients to you.

A Revolutionary Approach

One of the uses I like to make with Revolution is to create an interactive GUI application for the client. I create all the screen elements and embed them in an application. I send this application to the client so they can experiment with screen design. Each of these screen elements can be clicked and dragged around the screen. The code for that in revTalk is simply:

```
on mouseDown
    grab me
end mouseDown
```

That is all it takes. The simplicity of this code example is indicative of how easy and English-like the revTalk syntax is.

By programming with Revolution, I am able to develop software applications faster and more efficiently. Software maintenance and iterative changes are also made much easier. There is less in-code documentation required with revTalk because the English-like syntax is almost self-documenting. Over the years, we have developed a strong code base and reuse functions, commands, and behaviors often.

The Design and Development Process

We have well defined but flexible design and development processes. This formality is intended to ensure we do not overlook or breeze over a component in the design or development processes. Each project is unique and clients bring their own set of variables to bear on the process, making flexibility a critical component to the process. A typical process for a single eLearning game consists of the following phases:

- **Introduction Phase.** Initial dialogue to ensure we are the right team for our client and their project.
- **Needs Analysis Phase.** In understanding the client's needs, it is important to obtain detailed specifications from clients so we can develop exactly what they want.
- **Contracting Phase.** We negotiate a contract with our client that includes a detailed set of project milestones and pricing.
- **Design Phase.** We develop a prototype that demonstrates the software solution's layout and functionality. This is an iterative process allowing clients the ability to change and refine their ideas and requirements. As much as we would like to work from a master specification document, change is always part of any project.
- **Development Phase.** Here we develop the final application, one chunk at a time. We ask our clients to sign off on each chunk. This helps keep the project on schedule and allows our clients the "hands-on" oversight most desire.
- **Testing Phase.** Once all project chunks have been signed off, we produce a beta version of the application at which time functionality is locked. We put the program through extensive QA/bug testing and provide it to the client for their own testing.
- **Refine & Release Phase.** Here we fix any programming anomalies that were discovered in the Testing Phase, make final refinements, and release the final version of the software.
- **Maintenance Phase.** We typically provide twelve months of free bug fixes in case any were missed prior to release.

Chapter Six

What Else You Should Know

The quest for knowledge regarding how to research, establish, maintain, and grow a software consulting business is never-ending. The previous five chapters provided all the essentials. This chapter adds to that foundation of knowledge with additional insights into important issues that you should consider before you create your consulting business and while you manage it.

Seven Deadly Traps of Software Consulting

Seven Deadly Traps? That seems a bit dramatic, I know, but you do not want to fall into any of these traps.

Trying To Do It All

New consultants often want to take on every job and every client they can acquire. This might be a method to generate quick revenue, but the lack of focus this causes can result in quality loss. Each client should be looked upon as a long-term client—beyond the current project. This means you and your team need to give sufficient attention to your client and complete focus to the software solution you are developing for them.

There is also the danger of spreading your assets too thin when you take on more projects than you should at once. These assets include your time, your team's time, hardware assets, conference lines, and so on.

Another aspect of trying to do it all is to take on projects in which you do not have expertise. Just because a client is willing to award a contract to you does not mean you should accept it. Unless you are confident that you will be able to outsource skills that your team does not have, stay away from these contracts.

The remedy for this trap is to take it slow and be cautious.

Financial Simplicity

People that start their own consulting business with no other employees or partners usually use their personal banking accounts to support their business. This makes things simple, but it is not advisable. Setting up a separate set of bank or credit union accounts is affordable, easy, and will make it easier for you at tax time. Keep your business and personal banking separate from one another. You can easily transfer money between the accounts to pay yourself or to provide additional seed money. Contact your current bank or credit union for their business account requirements and schedule of fees. You will be surprised how affordably easy it is to avoid the financial simplicity trap.

Keeping the IRS at Bay

If you run your business in the United States, you are subject to income tax withholdings. Your clients are not going to deduct federal income tax withholdings when they pay you. This puts the burden of paying that tax on you. There are rules, rates, and penalties that you should learn about early on in the formation of your consultancy. Consulting with an accountant or a tax attorney is in your best interest.

Sales tax is an issue that is handled by your state. If you end up creating a product that you sell, you will want to contact your county office representing the state's secretary of state. Again, this is information you should discover before your first sale.

Avoiding the Law

It is a common trap to ignore legal matters when new consultants get started. Consulting with a lawyer or legal service will pay tremendous dividends down the road. You can search for a local lawyer, consult Elance.com for a freelance lawyer, or use a legal service such as LegalZoom.com. Here are some legal issues that you should consider:

- Trademarks
- Patents
- Copyrights
- Incorporation
- LLC formation
- Legal documents
- Contracts
- Partnership agreements

Growing Too Rapidly

Most consultants hope for growth, but few are ready for rapid growth. If you are handling three active projects at full capacity, what happens if you bid on and are awarded six additional contracts? That would mean your active projects would require you to work at 300 percent capacity. This is impossible, so your options are to: (1) do each project with less than optimal effort; (2) fail at one or more projects; (3) extend delivery dates; or (4) hire additional people to handle the extra work. The only real option here is number (4), hiring additional people to handle the extra work.

Your best action in this situation is to hire freelancers to augment your team. It takes time to find and vet freelancers, and you might not have a lot of time before work on a project is set to begin. Ideally, you will not take on more projects than your firm can handle at once. Also, as you work with freelancers, add them to your network and let them know you would like to use them again for specific tasks in the future. This gives you a talent pool ready to help when needed.

The Name Mistake

Some consultants do not spend much time picking a name for their company. It is very common for people to use their own name. While there is no problem with this, it might hinder your future growth. If your name is Ted Batch, you could name your company Ted Batch Consulting. If you grow into new markets and your team is a couple of dozen strong, do you still want Ted Batch Consulting to be your firm's name? You might, and that is okay. If you would rather a name that is more appropriate for a larger consulting firm, then you should start with that name in the beginning.

Changing your company's name and branding is possible, but a hassle that can be avoided with enough prior planning.

Outsourcing Treatment

It is extremely common for software consultants to use freelancers for skills and services the consultancy does not have organically. The deadly trap here is to mistreat the freelancers. Mistreating freelancers is not a wide-spread problem, but it does occur. There is a trend of treating freelancers as disposable assets.

Think who these freelancers are. They are really just like you. You are staring your own software consulting business. The freelancers you will employ will have their own consultancies as well. Sure, you are paying the bills and are in charge of the project, but that does not give you license to mistreat other freelancers. You can remain in charge without beating your chest, talking down to people, or being dishonest.

Let's take an example. For Project Kiwi (this is not real), you hire four freelancers: a graphic artist, a researcher, an animator, and a programmer. You explain to each of them that the project is scheduled for eighteen months and you will require an average of twenty-five hours per week of their services. If this were what you projected and communicated to them, then I would hope that you really have an average of twenty-five hours of work for each of them over the next eighteen months. The freelancers will count on the twenty-five hours of work each week, understanding that some weeks will be shorter and others longer. This means they will not accept other projects that will compete with your project. If you start having internal problems, you realize your time estimates were wrong, or the requirements have changed, you owe it to the freelancers to communicate this to them. Although they are not full members of your staff, they are, in essence, part-time employees.

If you use freelancers, think if you could be as successful without them. The answer is mostly likely "no." So, it is worth the effort for you to treat them with dignity and respect. Hold their feet to the fire, offer negative and positive feedback, pay them on time, be honest with them, and treat them as an integral part of your team.

LEGAL MATTERS

Legal disclaimer: consult with a lawyer or legal service before taking any of these steps. This section is intended to give you some insight into legal matters, not to offer legal advice.

There are several legal concerns for software consultants. The primary concerns are what form your business will take, trademarks, patents, and copyrights, contracts, and warrantees.

What Form Should Your Business Take

There are two basic options here. You can incorporate your business (e.g., Silver Lining Consulting, Inc.) or establish your business as a Limited Liability Company (LLC) (e.g., Silver Lining Consulting LLC). Each form of establishment has benefits.

By incorporating your business, you can formally separate your personal assets from your company's liabilities. If you are sued, your personal assets cannot be touched. Obtaining business loans is reportedly easier for businesses that are incorporated than for other forms of businesses. There are also tax benefits for incorporated businesses.

Establishing your business as a Limited Liability Company (LLC) has similar benefits to that of an incorporated business but without the overhead that comes with managing a corporation. There are tax benefits to being an LLC as well. Regarding taxation as an LLC, there are options such as pass-through entity status. Consult a lawyer or legal service for more information.

Trademarks

You can protect your business name and its logo by registering a trademark with the United States Patent and Trademark Office (URL: http://www.uspto.gov/trademarks). There are lawyers that specialize in this area and several great legal services that can handle this for you for a nominal fee. Trademarks are valid for ten years and are renewable.

Patents

Obtaining a patent will help you prevent others from using your works without your permission. Patents are secured through the United States Patent and Trademark Office (URL: http://www.uspto.gov/patents). Like with trademarks, there are lawyers that specialize in this area and several great legal services that can handle this for you for a nominal fee. Patents are valid for twenty years from the date the application was filed.

Copyrights

Copyrighting your original work will protect it from being reproduced or reused without your permission. Copyright laws are complex and often misunderstood. You can learn everything you wanted to know about copyrights and copyright law at the United States Copyright Office (URL: http://www.copyright.gov). A great start is to review their "Copyright Basics" document at: http://www.copyright.gov/circs/circ1.pdf.

It is not necessary to register copyrighted works with the U.S. Copyright Office. In fact, original works are automatically copyrighted from the date of creation. It is still a good idea to register your copyrights with the U.S. Copyright Office. This provides an official record of your copyrights and makes any related legal actions easier.

There is no requirement to include a copyright notice on your work, even if it is copyrighted. U.S. law no longer requires this, but it is a good idea to include a copyright notice when possible.

As you probably expect, there are lawyers that specialize in this area and several great legal services that can handle this for you for a nominal fee. Copyrights are valid for the duration of the author's life plus seventy years.

Contracts

Contract law can be very complicated. Lawyers use their own version of the English language, which is not always the easiest to decipher. Using a lawyer or legal service to generate your contracts and review the ones presented to you is a smart business decision.

The basic elements of a contract are the agreement, consideration, performance/delivery, capacity, legality, and reality of consent. The agreement must be mutual between both parties. The consideration should include obligation from both parties, thereby tying both parties to the contract. The performance/delivery is the detailing of what each party must perform or deliver. For example, party A must pay $12,500 for services provided by party B. Capacity refers to the legality of the two parties being able to enter into the contract. Legality refers to whether or not the contract is actually legal. Lastly, reality of consent protects both parties from fraud.

Seek the assistance of a lawyer before signing your name on the dotted line.

Warrantees

Warrantees are written assurances you provide to your clients with regard to the software solutions you deliver. Be careful how you word the warrantee; you might be signing yourself up for a lot of free work.

Tax Concerns

If there were one area that new consultants often neglect the most, it would be tax related issues. Your firm's business form (i.e., LLC or Inc.) will determine much of your tax-related requirements. If your company has a chief operations officer (COO), then s/he should become very familiar with tax laws, reporting requirements, authorized deductions, authorized write-offs, record keeping requirements, and employee-related tax issues.

Do not make assumptions about your car, depreciation, or book keeping. According to IRS reports, the number one reason small businesses fail tax audits is due to poor record keeping. Saving receipts, invoices, and other documents related to monies, purchases, and billing will help you complete tax documents more accurately and could be a big help should you get audited. Keep your documents in a safe place and organized. How you organize your tax documents is not as important as ensuring they are indeed organized. Categories could include automotive, employee salaries, facilities, marketing, equipment, software, professional publications, entertainment, travel, and so on.

You should become familiar with the IRS 1099 Misc Form, which is a way earned income, can be documented. The folks at Guru.com and Elance.com offer 1099 service for free. They issue you a single 1099 at the end of the year to help you with your income tax filing.

In certain cases, you could be required to pay quarterly taxes instead of waiting until the end of the tax year. Consulting with an accountant, tax attorney, the IRS, or a legal service can save you a lot of hassle and money.

OTHER OPPORTUNITIES

The United States Small Business Administration's Office of Technology manages two programs that represent potential opportunities for consultants: the Small Business Innovation Research (SBIR) program and the Small Business Technology

Transfer (STTR) program. Eleven federal departments submit research and development opportunities via the SBIR program and another five departments use the SSTR program for research and development.

Competing for contracts via the SBIR and SSTR programs is extremely competitive and equally lucrative. It does not cost anything to submit proposals and the process is fairly straightforward. Visit the http://www.sbir.gov Web site for details.

CASE STUDY: PART VI

This is the concluding part of our continuing case study. The issues presented in this chapter are ones that I heeded early on. In brief:

- I used Legal Zoom to register my trademark and for establishing my LLC and DBA.
- I document and organize financial records.
- I use professional tax services.

Outsourcing Treatment

I am a freelancer and also use freelancers. I truly treat freelancers I employ with the same dignity and respect that I expect from my employers. This goes a long way in obtaining great results and establishing long-standing professional relationships.

One outsourcing horror story worth mentioning is a contract I had with an employer for an average of thirty hours per week. At weekly meetings, freelancers—I was one of many—were given tasks to complete for that week. One week, I went over the thirty hours and was publicly reprimanded. My years of military service told me that was inappropriate—we praise in public and discipline in private. In any case, I was only performing the assigned work, and not at a slow pace.

This incident taught me, at least with that employer, to be mindful of the time spent each week and stop work if it I was in danger of exceeding the limit. This caused some things to slip, but the employer did not mind. Oddly, I later averaged over fifty hours a week for ten consecutive weeks for the same employer because of a lack of planning on their part. This is not a fair position in which to put a freelancer. You should plan your work in a manner that keeps it around the hours you agreed upon. Doubling a freelancer's time for a couple of weeks is sure to disrupt their personal and professional lives and make them less likely to work for you in the future.

The story continues...I experienced a nineteen-week period where I averaged less than eight hours per week—again, with the same employer. There was no breach of contract here, and several freelancers had similar experiences. What was lacking, and what I hope will help guide you, is that the employer did not do a good job in communicating these changes. Instead, freelancers were left wondering what had happened, how long this would last, and if it was a result of something they did or did not do.

In my case, I moved on to other clients. This, in the long run, was much better for my firm and me.

AFTERWORD

Writing a book on a topic like software consulting is like raising a child; it seems that you are never done. Every week, I learn something new or have a better understanding of previous knowledge. Nonetheless, the book would never be published if I waited until I knew everything—that day will never come. With that sentiment, I finalize this book, knowing there is so much more to learn.

It is my truest hope that this book helped someone. I know it would have helped me if it were written before I became a software consultant. You can visit this book's Web site, which contains a blog of updated information, links to great resources relevant to software consulting, and information on any future releases. That URL is:

www.softwareconsultingbook.com

If you want to contact me, please visit one of my consultancy Web sites: www.idleaders.com and www.three19.com.

Best,
Ed

Glossary

CAP - Collaborative Agile Production software

Cloud Computing - Computer services provided virtually over the Internet

Cloud Storage - Data stored on servers via the Internet

Consultant - Expert adviser

COO - Chief Operating Officer

DBA - Doing Business As

ECSA - Electronic Collaborative Software Application

eZine - Electronic magazine

FFP - Fixed Full Price

FP - Fixed Price

Freelancer - Self-employed professional

GUI - Graphical User Interface

IM - Instant Messenger / Instant Messaging / Instant Message

INC - Incorporated / Incorporated Corporation

Listserv - Electronic mailing list (List Server)

LLC - Limited Liability Company

MySQL - Relational database management system

NGO - Non-Governmental Organization

Niche - Subset of a market

Open Source - Freely available source code

PDF - Portable Document Format

PIP - Project Information Portal

RFP - Request for Proposal

SAAS - Software As A Service

SBIR - Small Business Innovation Research program

Screencast - Recording of a computer's audio and video (screen recording)

SEO - Search Engine Optimization

SMS - Short Message Service

SQL - Structured Query Language

STTR - Small Business Technology Transfer program

UI - User Interface

URL - Uniform Resource Locator

Virtual Team - A team that is not geographically co-located

VOIP - Voice Over Internet Protocol

Webinar - Web conferencing / presentations